# One Lucky Duck

Written by
**Alison Maloney**

Illustrated by
**Martha Lightfoot**

little bee

Down on the farm,
by the splishy, splashy pond,
**ONE** unlucky duck is sad.

"I've lost my quack
and **I** want to have it back."

So one unlucky duck
waddles through
the puddles and dives
into the duck pond.

But the quack is nowhere to be found.

Down on the farm,
in the slippy, sloppy muck,
the unlucky duck clucks.

**TWO** helpful hens say,
"ducks don't cluck."
"But **I**'ve lost my quack.
Can you help me get it back?"

So one unlucky duck
and two helpful hens
hunt in the hen house.

But the quack is nowhere to be found.

**3**

Down on the farm,
in the soggy, doggy yard,
the unlucky duck barks.

THREE dozy dogs say,
"ducks don't bark."
"But I've lost my quack.
Can you help me get it back?"

So one unlucky duck
and three dozy dogs
climb in the kennel.

But the quack is nowhere to be found.

Down on the farm,
on the slippy, slidy lawn,
the unlucky duck miaows.

FOUR cunning cats say,
"ducks don't miaow."
"But I've lost my quack.
Can you help me get it back?"

So one unlucky duck
and four cunning cats
file into the farmhouse.

But the quack is nowhere to be found.

**5**

Down on the farm,
in the prickly, tickly hay,
the unlucky duck neighs.

**FIVE** happy horses say,
"ducks don't neigh."
"But **I**'ve lost my quack.
Can you help me get it back?"

So one unlucky duck
and five happy horses
search in the stables.

But the **quack** is nowhere to be found.

Down on the farm,
on the bumpy, lumpy straw,
the unlucky duck honks.

SIX gabbling geese say,
"ducks don't honk."
"But I've lost my quack.
Can you help me get it back?"

So one unlucky duck
and six gabbling geese
stamp in the straw.

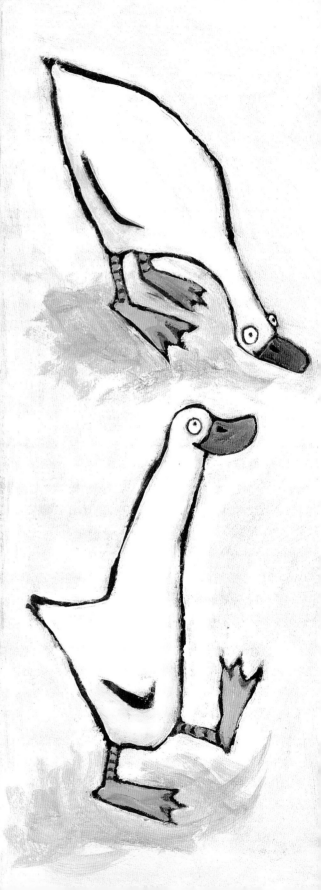

But the quack is nowhere to be found.

# 7

Down on the farm,
in the soggy, boggy field,
the unlucky duck baas.

SEVEN shaggy sheep say,
"ducks don't baa."
"But I've lost my quack.
Can you help me get it back?"

So one unlucky duck
and seven shaggy sheep
grub in the grass.

But the quack is nowhere to be found.

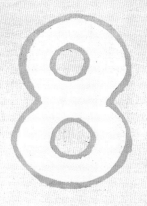

Down on the farm,
in the messy, mossy pen,
the unlucky duck bleats.

EIGHT gambolling goats say,
"ducks don't bleat."
"But I've lost my quack.
Can you help me get it back?"

So one unlucky duck
and eight gambolling goats
poke around the pen.

But the quack is nowhere to be found.

Down on the farm,
in the creaky, leaky barn,
the unlucky duck moos.

NINE clever cows say,
"ducks don't moo."
"But I've lost my quack.
Can you help me get it back?"

So one unlucky duck
and nine clever cows
cause chaos in the cowshed.

But the **quack** is nowhere to be found.

**10**

Down on the farm,
in the splishy, splashy pond,
ten dappled ducks quack 'STOP!
You won't find a quack like that.'

So, **TEN** dappled ducks,
**NINE** clever cows,
**EIGHT** gambolling goats,
**SEVEN** shaggy sheep,
**SIX** playful pigs,
**FIVE** happy horses,
**FOUR** cunning cats,
**THREE** dozy dogs and
**TWO** helpful hens say...

# "QUACK!"

...and one lucky duck
quacks back.

# "Quack!"

For Jim,
with love.

A.M.

 For Rosie and Jonny
and the Florio family.

M.L.

First published in 2005 by Meadowside Children's Books
185 Fleet Street, London, EC4A 2HS

This edition published in 2007 by Little Bee,
an imprint of Meadowside Children's Books
©Illustrations by Martha Lightfoot 2005

The right of Martha Lightfoot to be identified
as the illustrator of this work has been asserted
by her in accordance with the Copyright,
Designs and Patents Act, 1988

A CIP catalogue record for this book
is available from the British Library
Printed in Thailand

10 9 8 7 6 5 4 3 2